The Leaning Tree

by

James W. Reed

The contents of this work, including, but not limited to, the accuracy of events, people, and places depicted; opinions expressed; permission to use previously published materials included; and any advice given or actions advocated are solely the responsibility of the author, who assumes all liability for said work and indemnifies the publisher against any claims stemming from publication of the work.

All Rights Reserved
Copyright © 2019 by James W. Reed

No part of this book may be reproduced or transmitted, downloaded, distributed, reverse engineered, or stored in or introduced into any information storage and retrieval system, in any form or by any means, including photocopying and recording, whether electronic or mechanical, now known or hereinafter invented without permission in writing from the publisher.

Dorrance Publishing Co
585 Alpha Drive
Pittsburgh, PA 15238
Visit our website at *www.dorrancebookstore.com*

ISBN: 978-1-4809-4431-2
eISBN: 978-1-4809-4454-1

The Leaning Tree

The mighty conifer was incredibly tall. So tall, in fact, he could easily see beyond the reaches of the vast forest...

At the leading edge of the woods where he grew, the rolling hills stretched out mile after mile, to meet the snowcapped mountains.

"Spectacular! What a *view*," thundered the colossal giant. "It must be my job to protect and preserve all that I see." But,

when his loud voice rumbled, the ground would shake and crumble, completely annoying every living thing around him.

"Hey, put a cork in it!" barked a handsome, boldly striped birch tree. "Somebody really ought to cut that braggart down to size," he angrily insisted.

"Oh sure, no problem, piece of cake," scoffed his friend, a wise, stately red oak. "And just who do you suppose is gonna do that?" he asked.

"How should I know?" replied the birch.

"Beats me."

"Never mind!" snapped the oak, shaking loose the last of his bulging, brown acorns. "And don't bother complaining anymore 'cause there's nothing you or I or anyone else can do about it."

Nevertheless, the towering pine stood straight and tall above them all and it remained that way for an age or two until…

One cool autumn evening, a great tempest swept down from the north. Fierce winds howled through the forest, lashing at the defenseless trees.

Suddenly, without warning, a bolt of lightning flashed from a dark cloud, striking the proud giant upon his crown. In one swift stroke, he was chopped in two, while his top half - still smoldering from the heat – came crashing to the ground.

Still, the wind and rain grew stronger. And down below, the damp soil started to buckle all around his massive roots. Slowly, but steadily, the big tree began to lean...

"TIMBERRR!" bellowed the frightened giant. "GOIN DOWN!" Then rather abruptly,

the violent storm passed, leaving the forest in a deathly, black silence...

Upon first light the following day, a thick fog clung heavily to the wet, sagging trees. Everywhere, branches and limbs littered the forest floor. Yet, no one suffered more than the mighty giant himself...

There he leaned, battered and broken, a half-soldier of the woods with a long, crooked scar burned into his side.

"Just look at me!" he groaned. "I'll *never* be king of this beautiful forest again."

When at last the other trees came to their senses, they turned to the stricken giant and showed no mercy.

"Wow! Get a load of you, big fella," shouted the old, weathered oak. "I can hardly believe my aging eyes," he said with a laugh. "But sure looks like someone or something just *popped-your-pinecones* for ya!"

"Yeah, serves you right," sneered the obnoxious birch. "You got real toasted friend, I mean like, *fried!*" An ugly chorus of taunting laughter echoed throughout the forest.

"I must paint a sorry, pitiful picture indeed!" thought the giant. "If only another wind would blow through and knock me down." But the wind did not. Instead, a cold, cruel winter set in and more ridicule came with it.

"You're nothing but a giant *eyesore*!" yelled a scrawny, little maple tree. "Not even the pure white snow looks good on you. You'd do much better to simply keel over and *rot*!" said the brat.

And though he agreed, the poor giant knew this was not possible, as his strongest and deepest roots were firmly

anchored in the earth. Gradually, inch by icy inch, the long winter melted away to greet the spring.

Large beasts and small critters busily roamed and scampered about. Colorful birds of bewildering variety sang joyfully from every treetop. And a billion buzzing insects filled the air.

It was a healthy, thriving woodland once more. Sadly, however, the animals took no notice of the tortured figure lurking in the shadows.

"Now I truly feel worthless," wept the giant.

"I'm afraid I shall *never* be happy again…"

Then, one bright, sunny afternoon, as the giant peered up to a blue patch of sky, he recognized a dark, gliding object he'd seen once before, a long time ago. His big heart beat faster…

Soaring high above the forest canopy, a keen-eyed creature was patiently studying the trees below. Finally, with a sharp, piercing call, she circled towards the slumping conifer. Pulling back her broad, powerful wings, she gently landed.

Shortly after, her splendid mate joined her atop the giant's charred and splintered trunk. This tree was indeed the *perfect* place for the magnificent eagles to build their fortress.

Wasting no time, the persistent pair began carrying aloft the numerous sticks and branches that had fallen during the storm. One by one, they were carefully arranged. And day, by passing day, the sturdy structure grew.... And it GREW!

In spellbound astonishment, the entire forest watched as the eagles revealed their masterpiece...

A glorious, incredible new crown resting proudly upon the humble shoulders of the leaning tree.

And, as the noble birds tended their precious white eggs, the mighty giant knew at last what he was chosen to protect...

His crown, this nest, fit for a king!

The End